G000149727

Welcome on board!
The Sea Stallion from Glendalough

A Viking longship recreated

The Viking Ship Museum, Roskilde 2007

Welcome on board! The Sea Stallion from

 The longship is the very essence of the Viking Age. It was with the aid of such ships that the Scandinavian lands were created. Across sounds and belts and along trackless coasts the long-ships carried warriors and discord – but also order and the power of the state and this led gradually to the Nordic kingdoms finding their places within Europe. It was also the longship that for a short period in the eleventh century formed a bridge across the North Sea that was strong enough to bind Norway, Denmark, South Sweden and England together in Canute the Great's North-Sea Empire. And it was the longship, often manned with mercenary forces, that ensured the Scandinavian immigrants and their successors continued political power and influence along the coast of Northern Europe, in Normandy, in England, in Scotland and in Ireland.

The SEA STALLION FROM GLENDALOUGH is the nearest that we can come today to experiencing a complete longship from the time when this type of ship reached its culmina-tion. At the same time the ship is an experiment. Here we are attempting with a confrontation between the reconstructed ship and the forces of nature to understand the prerequisites for the expansion of territory in the Viking Age. Trial voyages with the SEA STALLION tell us not only about travelling times and seaworthiness but also about the great demands that are made on gear and crew when sailing in an open ship across the North Sea.

The model for the SEA STALLION is an archaeological find, the Viking ship Skuldelev 2, that was excavated in 1962. It was originally built by Scandinavians in Dublin in the year 1042 but ended its life after many years service as a part of the barrier constructed 15 km north of Roskilde, the royal seat of Denmark at that time. Thanks to decades of research it has been possible to recon-struct both the original appearance of the ship and the methods that were employed by the shipbuilders in Dublin almost a thousand years ago.

This booklet invites you to explore the SEA STALLION and its history. Welcome on board!

Tinna Damgård-Sørensen
Director
The Viking Ship Museum

The Find

The archaeological model for the SEA STALLION was found at Skuldelev north of Roskilde in 1957. It was the second ship that the archaeologists found in the sea-route barrier and that is why it was called Skuldelev 2. The archaeological excavations were originally intended to be quite limited. It had always been known that there was a barrier at the place in question – and investigations of individual ship's parts that had been salvaged from the barrier had shown that it contained a vessel from the late Viking Age or the medieval period. Everyone expected, however, the ship to have been severely damaged. No one had dreamt of finding no fewer than five ships from the Viking Age or that the find would result in the establishment of what is today the Viking Ship Museum in Roskilde.

After a number of underwater investigations the Skuldelev ships were excavated in 1962. It was an epoch-making event. Never before had archaeologists been faced with a task of that magnitude – all the earlier ship-excavations had either been of graves on land or the salvaging of large, solid wrecks such as VASA, which had been raised in 1961 from the bottom of the Stockholm archipelago. At Skuldelev we had a matter of tens of thousands of shattered, soft and deformed pieces of wood that could hardly bare to be lifted and which crumbled and turned to dust if they were allowed to dry out. In every phase of the excavation new methods had to be developed.

Instead of attempting to salvage the find with the aid of divers under the water, the whole area with the barrier – 1,600 m² – was enclosed within a coffer dam and the water was pumped out. In the course of three summer months, during which the archaeologists more or less lived on the little artificial island in Roskilde Fjord, the five ships in the barrier were carefully exposed, photographed, raised, packed and brought in to land. To use shovels or spoons, as during excavations on land, was not feasible – the metal tools would all too easily have cut into the soft material. Instead the ships' parts were carefully cleaned with a gentle spray of water, while sand and shells were mostly removed with our bare hands. Over the whole excavation there hung a constant mist of water from the sprinklers whose task it was to keep everything wet and prevent damage to the timber by drying out. Waterproofs were the only conceivable clothing, whatever the weather.

Skuldelev 2, which was the model for the SEA STALLION, belongs to the second building-phase of the barrier. The ship had been filled with stones and sunk on top of two other vessels. Since it thus lay at the top of the barrier, exposed to the waves and damaged by ice in the cold winters, it was less well protected than the ships lower down in the barrier and was consequently the most badly damaged. It was in fact in such a bad condition

The Skuldelev blockage, built ca 1070.

SKULDELEV

ROSKILDE

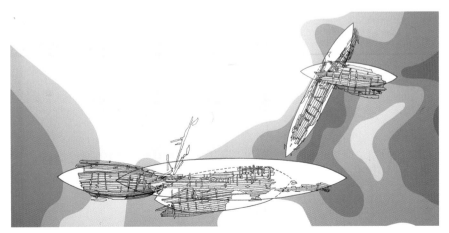

that the archaeologists thought they had found parts of two different ships so that part of Skuldelev 2 was christened Skuldelev 4 before the misunderstanding was cleared up. In the course of the excavation, however, it became clear that the hitherto longest longship from the Viking Age had been found. By good fortune it turned out that many of the most important parts of the ship had simply fallen down from the barrier as the ship gradually fell to pieces. And now it was lying awaiting excavation in the channel which the barrier had served to block.

In the course of the excavation all the ships' parts were carefully described, numbered and photographed and a photogrammetric survey was made of the whole excavation. In order to reconstruct the ships, however, it was necessary to carry out a very exact documentation. During the excavation the individual ships' parts were washed and packed in plastic and then sent to the conservation laboratory, where they were drawn at the scale 1:1. Every single edge or scratch, every single nailhole or sign of wear and tear was transferred carefully to drafting folio and the drawings were subsequently reduced to the scale of 1:10. Once the documentation of the shape and appearance of the objects was assured, it was possible to start work on the conservation.

The conservation offered a particular challenge. The many centuries at the bottom of the sea meant that bacteria had degraded most of the cells in the wood. Only the walls of the cells were left, held together by the water which with the passage of time had replaced what had been lost. At the very moment that the wood was allowed to dry out, the cells collapsed and the pieces were more or less transformed into dust. The final solution was to replace the water in the wood with an artificial wax, PEG (polyethylenglykol), which is soluble in water, mouldable when heated but firm at normal room temperature. By placing the wood in baths containing a PEG solution heated to 60° it was possible through the course of a number of years to replace the water with wax so that the ships' parts could be dried, assembled and put on exhibition.

What was the age of the ship and where had it come from? When the Skuldelev ships were excavated, the possibilities for scientific dating were limited to the so-called C14-method, which is not particularly precise with such young finds. At the same time all the ships had been completely emptied of all equipment before they were sunk and there were therefore no finds on board that could date them. At the end of the 1980s, however, a new dating method, dendrochronology, had become so reliable that we also ventured to use it on the Viking ships from Skuldelev. The method namely required that some of the planks of the ships had to be cut across. In 1990 the experiment was made with Skuldelev 2 and

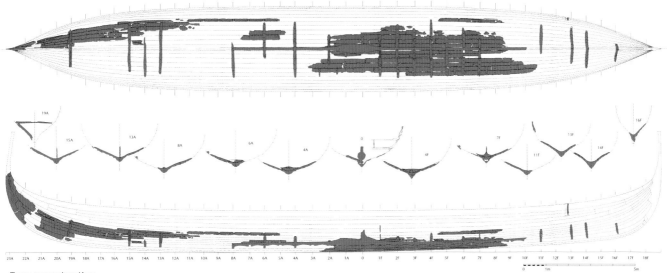

Torso reconstruction

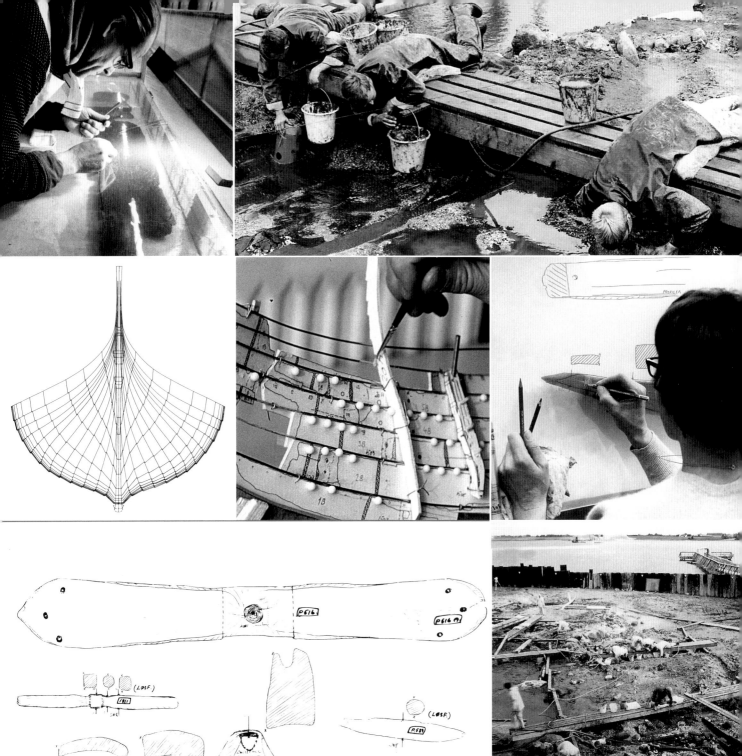

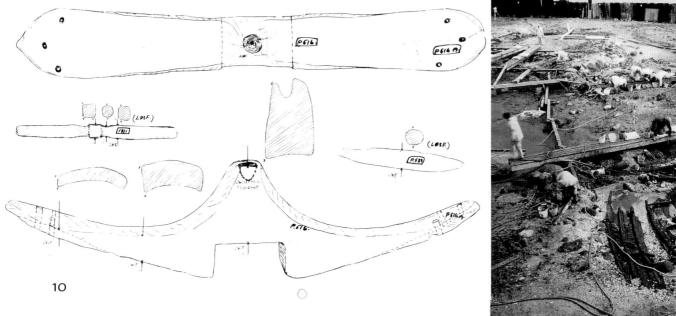

the result confirmed a suspicion already harboured by the archaeologists: The ship had indeed been built by Vikings but not in Scandinavia. The measurements of the annual growth rings in the planks revealed namely that they had been made from trees that had grown in the neighbourhood of Dublin in Ireland. The date when the ship was built could also be determined exactly: The keelson of the ship had been felled in the summer of 1042, by which time the construction of the ship must have been well under way.

Skuldelev is the one of the ships from which the least timber has been preserved. It is therefore also the one that has been most difficult to reconstruct. It was not until 1993 that the erection of the ship in the Viking Ship Museum could be brought to a conclusion, 31 years after its excavation. But even at that date some of the questions about the shape of the hull remained to be answered. One of the biggest problems concerned the determination of the length of the ship. No coherent parts of the ship have survived from fore to aft. With the exception of a few pieces of the frame-timbers, the forward part of the ship is lacking altogether. By transferring the reduced drawings of the ships' parts onto cardboard and fitting them together in the model it was possible to solve this problem. The model showed namely that the pieces could not be fitted together satisfactorily, if the length from stem to stem was less than 29.2 m. Conversely, the length could not be more than 31.2 m, if the ships lines were still to run evenly and harmoniously – a demand upon

which great emphasis was apparently placed in the Viking Age. Circumspection is a virtue, also among archaeologists, and the SEA STALLION is there- fore the expression of the shortest

possible reconstruction of Skuldelev 2 – it is 29.4 m long.

The work on the parts recovered led to a *torso reconstruction* but by no means all of the questions were answered. There was particular uncertainty about how the upper parts of the ship had been constructed. In order to study this the next step was to build a wooden model of the ship with a proposal as to how the missing parts may have looked. Comparisons were made with other, contemporary finds – that is to say mainly with the other Skuldelev ships – and the model offered the possibility of experimenting with various solutions before the building of a reconstruction in full scale was begun. It was not least for

the examination of the rigging that the model proved to be a significant tool.

In 2000 we could finally begin the construction of the SEA STALLION. The work on the recreation of Skuldelev 2 in full scale raised new questions and often gave us cause to consult the archaeological material. Which tools were used for the original building of the ship? How were they used? What did the most well-suited trees look like? What was the most expedient way to organise our work? The work on the reconstruction continued, now exploiting the practical experience of the boatbuilders in shaping the timber and planks and dealing with the nails and the cordage as the angle of attack.

The SEA STALLION was launched on 4th September 2004. The ship that was finally launched into its right element was the unique sum of many years of research. No one can guarantee that it looks precisely like the ship that was launched in Dublin in 1042 – but it is the very best bid that we can make today.

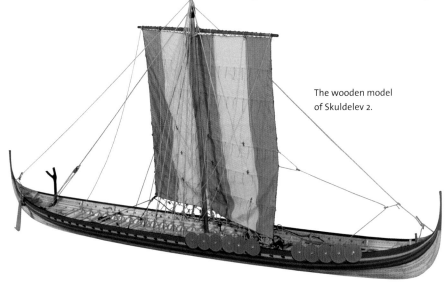

The wooden model of Skuldelev 2.

Keel and lot

The keel is the backbone of the longship. It has to be strong so that it can withstand stresses and strains at sea and when the ship is run up onto the beach. It also has to be flexible, however, so that it is not broken up by the movements of the ship in the waves. The Vikings called the longships 'serpents' – perhaps because it felt as though they twisted their way through the water. The SEA STALLION's keel is more than 25 m long and passes over into curved pieces of wood that form the transition into the stems.

On the large longships the keel was never formed in one piece stretching from stem to stem. This was in part because it was impossible to get hold of trees that were tall enough and in part because the keel did not have to be perfectly straight but had to swing upwards towards the ends. So even though only 7.6 m of the original keel of Skuldelev 2 is preserved, we can be almost certain that it was originally assembled from several pieces.

The keel of the SEA STALLION is made of three pieces: A central piece of a little under 18 m and an extension at each end. Between these and the stems curved pieces of timber, the *lot*s, were fitted to form a gentle transition between keel and stem.

The keel is very slender. Although it is over 25 m long, it is only 18 cm tall and at its broadest 22 cm. It has been constructed so that the pith of the wood is in the middle of the keel. In this way the shipbuilder avoids large knots and gets a strong keel. The garboards – the first row of planks on either side – stand almost on end. This makes the keel stiffer and gives the ship better sailing qualities – an advantage in the difficult waters of the Irish Sea.

Today it is not easy to find a perfect oak trunk that is 18 m tall in a Danish forest. We found the keel for the SEA STALLION in Skåningshave in Lolland. The keel from the biggest longship that has been discovered so far – incidentally in Roskilde harbour, just beside the Viking Ship Museum – would seem to have had the quite incredible length of 28 m. Even that keel received extensions at either end so that the whole ship was 36 m in length.

The joins in the keel are very important. The model for the *hagelasker*, hooked scarfs, with which the SEA STALLION's keel has been joined together, is taken from a warship from the end of the tenth century that was found in the harbour off Hedeby near Schleswig. Because the two parts of the join are hooked into each other, they are specially good at withstanding tension.

Hedeby

The stem

The fore- and after-stems are built in the same way in a Viking ship. Already in their shaping many of the lines of the ship and its qualities are determined. The work on the hewing and raising of the stems was among the most responsible tasks in the whole building process. We know that at the beginning of the thirteenth century the man who performed this task was known as a stafnasmiðr – a stem-smith. He was one of the most important and highest paid men working on the whole building process.

Each of the stems of the SEA STALLION is comprised of three parts. On Skuldelev 2 the two lower parts of the after-stem are preserved, together with a small fragment of the top one. They are all of oak. The stem is a stepped stem. This means that it is carved out in a series of steps to which the planks from the ship's sides are fastened. The stem is deeply hollowed out so that the planks can be fastened with clench nails instead of with spikes. On the side of the midmost stem-piece decorative mouldings have been carved so that it look as though the planks of the ship's sides continue right up to the tip of the stem. In reality most of

the planks come to an end some distance from the stem. It is namely not possible to make room for all the twelve strakes on the stem. A number of multiple hooding ends each fasten 2-3 planks to one of the steps in the stem. In the reconstruction we have made three multiple hooding ends on each side and let some planks run together into one even before they have reached the stem.

The joins between the various parts of the stem and between the stem and the lot are quite simple scarfs. It is only in the uppermost join between the middle piece and the rather decorative stem-top that the join has been given

a breast that makes it better suited for withstanding pressure. The top piece of the stem-point was not preserved so its shape has been reconstructed on the basis of illustrations of longship stems from the twelfth and thirteenth centuries and of small miniatures of stem-points from the same period that have been found in the Norwegian trading-port Bergen.

The stems of the warships were often ornamented with colours, with carved figures or with metal that could shine in the sun and it is often the stems that are shown in graffiti from the Viking Age. We do not know whether Skuldelev 2's stems were ornamented.

Skuldelev 2

Fortun Stave Church,, Norway

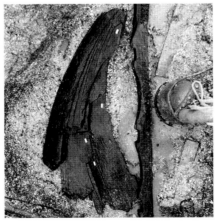

Bergen

The weather-vane

The function of the weather-vane on the prow of the ship is not to show the direction of the wind but to show who is coming. The gilded metal gleams and reflects itself in the sun so that already from a long distance away it can be seen that this is a particularly splendid vessel. The motifs depicted on the vane are those appropriate for a ruler, showing the battle between good and evil. The weather-vane sits loose so that it can be removed when the ship is not in use – or if one does not want to betray who is coming.

The weather-vane on the prow of the SEA STALLION is an exact copy of the one on Söderala church in Sweden. It is made of gilded copper and its shape shows that it must originally have been placed on the stem of a ship. The motif represents a largish animal – perhaps a lion – which is defending itself against a serpent and a smaller animal. It is made in the Ringerike-style, which was used in Scandinavia in particular in the period 1000-1050 – and for a rather longer period in Ireland, where it became very popular.

Such vanes to set up on the stems – *veðrviti* "weather-vanes" – are often referred to in saga texts from the Middle Ages, where they seem to have been part of the regular equipment of large warships. Three other examples – from Källunge church in Gotland and from Heggen and Tingelstad churches in Norway – show that the practice must have been rather widespread in the late Viking Age and the medieval period. This is also revealed by a small decorated stick showing a whole fleet of ships that was found in thirteenth-century layers in Bergen in Norway. Here it is clear that it is the largest and most important ships that bear such a decoration at the prow.

The original weather-vane from Söderala church in Helsingland is the most elaborately designed of the four. A lion crest adorns the top corner of the vane. The Källunge weather-vane derives from Gotland. Just like the vanes from Söderala and Heggen it is ornamented in the Ringerike-style and it has the same motif and gilding. The weather-vane from Tingelstad in Oppland is a slightly exotic creature compared to the others. From the point of view of the history of style it belongs to the second half of the twelfth century and its motifs are different. It shows David rescuing a lamb from the jaws of the lion and it is a dragon crest and not a lion that adorns the top corner of the vane.

Tingelstad

Källunge

Söderala

havhingsten fra glendalough

Gaudalen

The name

Scandinavian and Ireland meet in the name the SEA STALLION FROM GLENDALOUGH. The Vikings often used poetical metaphors – kennings – to describe the ships in their poetry. The SEA STALLION is our kenning for the recreated Irish longship. Glendalough is a valley in the Wicklow Mountains south of Dublin. Here in the Viking Age was found one of the most important monasteries in Ireland. In and around the hills there were great deciduous forests which provided the inhabitants of Dublin with timber for their houses, ships and fuel.

We only know a few names of ships from the Viking Age but the big ships at least would often seem to have been honoured in this way. The most famous is Olav Tryggvason's mighty warship, ORMR INN LANGI – "Orm the long", which he used at the sea battle near Svold in the year 1000. Another one of his ships was also called ORMR – but with the addition "inn skammi", "the short", while a third ship was called TRANA, "the crane". On the other side in the battle the Norwegian jarl Erik had a ship that was called BARÐI, a ship-name that probably referred to a particular shape of stem.

Among the few other ship-names that have been transmitted down to us in the scaldic verses we find St Olav's VISUNDR – "the Bison", and KARLHÖFÐI. This last name is perhaps a reference to the Emperor Charlemagne, who was Olav's great hero.

From William the Conqueror's Norman invasion fleet in 1066 we know the name of one ship, his flagship. His wife Matilda had had it built for him and given it the enigmatic name MORA. In Latin this would mean "Delay", a rather strange name for a ship. It is perhaps more likely that it was derived from Morini, the term for the inhabitants of Flanders, from where his wife came.

Three further ship-names from the Viking Age are known to us – although they are ships which have never sailed in real life. SKÍÐBLAÐNIR "assembled from pieces of thin wood" was the name of Frey's ship that could accommodate all the gods from Asgard and nevertheless could be folded up so that he could carry it in his pocket. NAGELFAR "nail ship" was the ship of the underworld. It was built from the toe- and finger-nails of dead men and was supposed to carry them to Ragnarok. HRINGHORNI "ship with a ring on the stem" was the biggest ship in the world and in this the body of the god Balder was burnt after his murder by Loki. Even though the Vikings in Ireland had become christianised long before Skuldelev 2 was built, they would undoubtedly have heard and retold the stories about these ships.

Oseberg

Glendalough

Bayeux

The side of the ship

The Viking ship is built like a strong, flexible shell that is shored up inside lengthwise and transversely. The quality of the strakes – the planks – in the bottom and sides of the ship is therefore crucial for the good qualities of the ship. In the SEA STALLION the planks are made of cloven oak and they are, as in all Viking ships, assembled so that the edges of the planks overlap each other – they are clinker built – and are held together with iron nails. The spaces between the planks are caulked with sheep's-wool and tar.

In some parts of Scandinavia the Viking-Age clinker-building technique has lived on to the present day, and the technique may go as far back as to the Bronze Age. In the oldest vessels, from the centuries before and around the Birth of Christ, the planks were sewn or lashed together, while iron nails make their appearance in the 2nd century after Christ. The memory of the sewn ships lived on, however. In Viking-Age scaldic poetry the sides of the ships, or even the whole ship, can be referred to as *súð*, "sewn", and the rows of iron nails on the sides of the ships are referred to by the term *saum* "seam". Most of the planks on the sides of the ship are *radially split*. This means that they are taken radially out of a large oak trunk, rather in the way one slices a cake or pie. In this way the cleaving takes place along the oaktree's silver-grain, the large cells that extend from the bark of the tree in towards its centre. Planks made in this way are very strong, but can only be made from very large and well-formed trunks. To make planks that are 33 cm broad you need a trunk that is 1 m in diameter. Such a trunk can give 16-24 strakes. For the SEA STALLION we used 14 trunks of this thickness, each of them 8-10 m long. After cleaving, the working up of the planks was done with axes. For these we used copies of finds from the Viking Age. Heavier axes with comparatively short edges were used for roughly hewing the material for the planks. For smoothing the surfaces use was made of a *T-shaped broadaxe* – an axe with a long edge that has only been ground from the one side – as known from the late Viking Age in both Denmark and the British Isles. We have used, among others, a copy of an axe found in Over Hornbæk in Denmark. It is very light and well suited for working up the radially split planks. It is also the T-shaped broadaxe that boatbuilders can be seen using in the Bayeux Tapestry, and in eleventh-century illustrations of the building of Noah's Ark.

Eleventh-century illustration of the building of Noah's Ark

Iron nails

The iron nails hold the ship's hull-shell together. Almost 8,000 nails were used on the ship and these were produced from about 450 kg of iron. Most of the nails were so-called clench nails, the Viking Age equivalents of nuts and bolts. They were used in particular for joining the planks together. Spikes or nails were only used where solid wood was to be nailed, for example to fasten the first strake or garboard to the keel.

None of the nails has been preserved in the original ship, Skuldelev 2 – they had rusted away long before the ship was excavated. It was with the aid of the impressions they had left in the timber, however, that it was possible for us to reconstruct what they must have looked like. The clench nails, which were the most numerous, consisted of a nail with a round head and a round 8-9 mm thick shank. First the nail would be hit through a previously bored hole in the planks. The end of the shank was pushed through a rove, a four-sided, approx. 28x28 mm plate with a hole in. The plate was positioned so that the edge was flush with the edge of the plank. The tip of

the shank would then be clipped off with a chisel and flattened down with a hammer – clenched – so that it arched out over the edges of the hole in the rove. In this way the rove was held fast and tightened in towards the timber. The spikes were made just like the clench nails except that they were pointed at the end and did not have a plate.

Analyses of the nails from other Viking ships have shown that a very low-carbon and pure iron was used for the nails. Iron such as this is both soft and ductile – two valuable qualities when the nails are to be clenched and when they need to last for a considerable time in a movable ship's hull like

the Viking ship's. It is also important that the iron does not contain other substances, since that might make it rust more quickly. If the nails are made of pure iron, they can last for up to 20 years. In order to protect them further we have chosen to dip them in tar while they were still ret-hot after forging.

To forge a single iron nail is not time-consuming but when enough nails are to be forged for a whole longship it is nevertheless a big – and rather mono-tonous – task. The smith had to spend several weeks forging the nails for the SEA STALLION.

Skuldelev 2

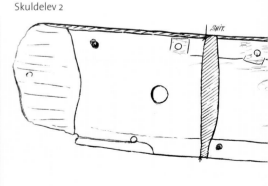

The tar

Wood tar is one of the oldest products for protecting wood that is known to man and some forms of tar were already being produced as early as in the Stone Age. Tar is extracted from the resinous materials that are produced by the trees themselves as a protection against bacteria and moulds. Many different kinds of wood can be used but pine is the best for the production of tar. For the construction of the SEA STALLION 600 litres of tar were required.

Tar gradually decomposes in salt water and is often only preserved as a yellowish substance on the ship finds. With the aid of infrared spectroscopy it is possible to determine which chemical materials this yellowish substance is made up of. This is done by subjecting a specimen to fluoroscopy with infrared light and measuring the light that it transmits. The result is a curve whose peaks and dips reflect various chemical substances. Analyses from the Skuldelev finds show that the ships were treated with a wood tar made from pine, perhaps with the addition of ochre.

There is also indirect evidence for the use of tar in Viking-Age navigation. During excavations in Hedeby almost a hundred tar-mops or -brushes have been found in the harbour that must have been used for tarring the ships. The mops were generally made by wrapping an old rag round a stick. In Hedeby's successor, Slesvig, large troughs have been found containing the remains of tar and with traces of a lid. The troughs were made of pine of a type that did not grow in the neighbourhood and they show that already soon after the Viking Age tar had become a trade commodity.

Today, wood tar is produced industrially but we had the tar for the SEA STALLION burnt in a stack in Finland. The raw material is resinous pine wood from trunks and roots that have been cloven into small sticks and carefully stacked. The complete stack is covered with turf and set alight and it has to be tended for several days while it is burning. The stack burns slowly from the outside and inwards and while burning the wood in the stack is heated up so that the tar substances are pressed out. They flow down into a large funnel and the tar runs through a pipe out under the stack to be drawn off. In order to produce 1,000 litres of tar it is necessary to burn 30 m^3 of wood and it is in particular the work involved in digging up the roots and hewing the wood that has taken the time. It took two to three thousand hours to produce 1,000 litres of tar.

Tar trough, Slesvig

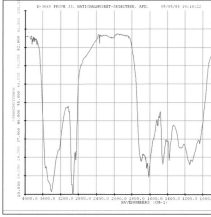

The colours

A longship is meant to signal power and wealth and this was done by decorating it in clear colours on hull and sail. The SEA STALLION is painted red, yellow and blue, which are colours that William the Conqueror's fleet is shown with in the Bayeux Tapestry. The pigments for Viking-Age paint could have come from far away or they can have been produced from native plants and minerals. The colours in the SEA STALLION are made of yellow and red ochre and the blue plant-dye indigo.

Certain traces of paint have not been found on the Skuldelev ships but they have been found on several other finds of Viking ships. The Gokstad ship was decorated with yellow and black, while on the Ladby ship it has been possible to distinguish remains of blue, yellow, red and green paint. The often coloured sails may have been sewn with coloured cloth or they may have been painted. Coloured paint is made by mixing one or more pigments in a binding material. As binding material we have used linseed oil, which is made of flax seeds and which we know was used in the Viking Age. The yellow colour can be made from orpiment "gold pigment", which is highly poisonous and which the Vikings imported from the Middle East and employed – for example on the Gokstad ship. It can also be made – and much more cheaply – from yellow ochre, a ferruginous mineral that is found naturally in many places and which was certainly employed in the Middle Ages. A red colour can be made from red ochre, which can both be found in nature and produced by heating up yellow ochre. Black can be made by mixing soot or crushed charcoal in the binding material and white from the poisonous pigment white lead. The blue pigment is the most difficult of all to obtain. The Vikings may have made it with crushed lapis lazuli, a semi-precious stone that had to be imported from the Middle East. It was cheaper to use the pigment indigo blue which is found both in the subtropical indigo-plant and in the naturalised plant woad, which they most certainly employed. In scaldic verses it is sometimes emphasised that the sail is coloured blue – perhaps it was considered to be a particularly prestigious colour because it was particularly expensive. We have coloured the SEA STALLION's sail yellow and red with ochre but the sail could also have been coloured with vegetable dyes.

Ochre　　　　Flax　　　　Woad　　　　Bayeux tapestry

A floor-timber

The floor-timbers form the lowest part of the frames, which are the ship's transverse reinforcement. They shore up the planks of the bottom of the ship which are fastened with nails of willow. The timbers are shaped to have minimum weight and maximum flexibility, just enough to withstand the forces exacted under sail. Although they lie hidden under the *dørk*, the ship's loose deck planks, they are nevertheless decorated with ornamental mouldings along the edges.

A characteristic feature of the Viking-Age ships is the way in which the frames are built up. They consist of at the bottom a floor-timber that stretches over an equal number of planks on either side of the ship. Over that lies a horizontal beam, a *bite*. The floor-timber and the *bite* are not nailed to each other but only to the strakes. They can therefore move slightly in relation to each other without damaging or splitting the strakes in the planking when the ship twists itself in the sea. The floor-timber is for the same reason not fastened to the keel.

Out of the original 38 floor-timbers in Skuldelev 2, 17 have been preserved. They are all of oak. Above the keel they are narrow and tall, while they become low and broad where they abut the bottom of the ship. During the construction of the ship the floor-timbers were put in position as soon as the lowermost strakes had been fixed. In this way they contribute to stabilising the hull as work continues. In order to give the necessary strength they need to be fitted extremely carefully. On the original find it is possible to see that the Viking-Age shipbuilder used his axe for this task and we did this, too. In the hand of a skilled craftsman the axe is a very precise tool.

The floor-timbers are fastened with treenails of willow that neither breaks nor splits easily. The treenails have a head on the outside, while on the inside they are locked with a wedge of oak or pine. The floor-timbers are hewn of oak that has grown naturally in the same shape as the finished floor-timber so that the fibres of the timber follow the shape of the floor-timber Presumably the Viking-Age landscape was rich in short oaktrees with strong branches that offered good timber for shipbuilding. In modern forests naturally grown timbers are often found high up in the crown of the trees and they get damaged when the tree is felled. We therefore had to climb to the top of many trees to cut off pieces of timber before the tree was felled.

Skuldelev 2

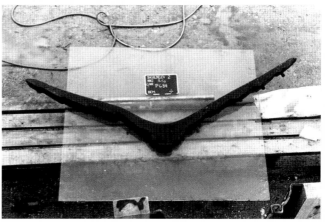

An intermediate frame

In between the SEA STALLION's regular frames the slender intermediate frames cling to the side of the ship. The apparently insignificant pieces of timber play an important role in the longships, where they reinforce the transition between the bottom and side of the ship and play their part in strengthening it without jeopardising its flexibility.

Parts of 22 intermediate frames from Skuldelev 2 were preserved but no complete examples. Most of them were found as loose pieces of timber but a few were still in position on the planking. On the well-preserved stern section of the planking it could be seen that intermediate frames were not employed right out at the ends of the ship – they were chiefly reinforcements for the long, almost equally broad central part of the hull. The intermediate frames began at the upper edge of the 4th strake, and a recess on the under side of the longitudinal reinforcement, the stringer, on the 7th strake shows that they must have passed underneath this. Some of the intermediate frames

consist of two pieces and it is therefore certain that they must have reached somewhat higher up on the side of the ship. In our reconstruction we have brought them to a conclusion under the stringer on the 9th strake.

The intermediate frames are only about 20 mm thick where they are thinnest. They are fastened to the planking with clench nails at both ends and in the middle. Along the edges there are decorative mouldings and the form of the frames is very elegant: narrow and slender in the middle and wider towards either end. The preserved ends are either cut off straight or shaped to a point so that they resemble most of all a modern necktie. Most of the preser-

ved intermediate frames are of oak but there are a few that are made of willow.

The two other large longships which we know from the Viking Age also have intermediate frames. In the longship from Hedeby we note, as in Skuldelev 2, that they are used in the central part but not at the ends, while a similar observation cannot be made in the sparsely preserved Roskilde 6.

Neither the 18 m-long Skuldelev 5 ship nor the Ladby ship measuring 21.5 m had intermediate frames and it would appear that such frames belong to the really big longships. Intermediate frames, but in a much sturdier version, are also found in the merchant ships of the Viking Age.

Hedeby

Roskilde 6

Skuldelev 2

Stringers

On the inside of the shell of the hull several longitudinal pieces of wood called stringers are fitted. They strengthen the hull and lock together its various parts. There are four of them on each side. The one lowest down is placed over the end of the floor-timbers, just above the floor. The second one is placed slightly higher up and the two together hold in position the *biti* and form the basis for the thwarts. The two stringers higher up lock the thwarts in position from above and strengthen the gunwale.

The longitudinal reinforcements in Skuldelev 2 have only been sparsely preserved but their shape could be reconstructed with the aid of the joggles and impressions left on the timber of the frames. In a longship the longitudinal reinforcements are very important because they help to control the flexibility of the ship. In the long midship section they were constructed more solidly in order to make the ship stiffer, while out towards the ends it was possible to make them thinner or omit them altogether. Just like the keel and the keelson the stringers had to be able to withstand tension so as far as possible they were made out of one piece of timber. One of the few preserved pieces shows us that when they were put together of several different pieces, hooked scarfs were employed in the joints.

The stringers were made of whole tree stems that were split into four pieces. Each piece could then be hewn out into one stringer. As with the planks and the floor-timbers, it was important to respect the grain of the wood while hewing – rather a slightly uneven but strong stringer than one that was fine and smooth but might break once the ship was under way.

Flexibility was a central element in Scandinavian shipbuilding in the Viking Age. The ships were – one might say with some slight exaggeration – not built to withstand the waves but to yield to them. Their shell construction was very well suited for this. Thanks to the strong cloven planks and the thousands of iron nails that held them together, the ship could withstand twisting in the waves. Other shipbuilding traditions were different and we do not know whether the Scandinavian shipbuilders deliberately tried to build flexible ships or whether the flexibility was so to say the result of their shipbuilding technique and they just had to live with it. Contemporary poets, however, reflect the technique when they refer to the ships as serpents and snakes.

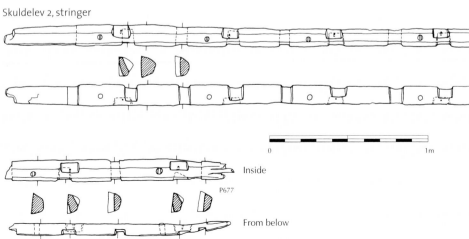

Skuldelev 2, stringer

Inside

P677

From below

A *rum*

Viking-Age warships were divided into *rum*. A *rum* consists of the distance between two frames. In each *rum* there was normally space for two men, who at the same time were responsible for operating an oar on either side of the ship. The *rum* formed a framework around a considerable part of the life of the crew during a voyage. It was here they worked, here they slept and if the ship got involved in a battle, it was perhaps here that they died. The *rum* in Skuldelev 2 was unusually small – this meant that there was space for more men in the ship.

The division of the Scandinavian ships into *rum* can be traced right back to the oldest clinker-built ships, the Nydam boats from South Jutland. They were built in the first centuries after the Birth of Christ and their only means of propulsion was with oars. Although the frame system was not yet so highly developed, the rowers here also sat on thwarts, which formed a part of the frames. In the three ships from Nydam, however, they had more room than in Skuldelev 2 – instead of only 73 cm there was a good metre between the frames. Other longships from the Viking Age are also less generous with space than the Iron-Age ships – here there is 80-90 cm to each *rum*. The very short distance between the frames of Skuldelev 2 forced the crew to row with small, short strokes.

None of the original *thwarts* or *thwart-knees* were preserved in Skuldelev 2 so those in the SEA STALLION are shaped on the model from the longship from Hedeby harbour. The thwarts have been constructed to be strong and light rather than to be comfortable! They are only 8-10 cm broad, have a lightly convex surface and they are fastened at each end with beautifully shaped knees. The thwarts themselves were quite straight and could have been made of material left over from the construction of the planks of the ship.

Dørken – that is to say the floor – in Skuldelev 2 was missing at the time of the excavation and must have been removed before the ship was sunk in the blockage. We can, however, work out what it must have looked like because one of the beams, *biter*, upon which it lay, still survives. This shows that *dørken* was built of loose, short pieces of planking that lay lengthwise in the ship. Under *dørken* the crew could stow away their gear. A plank from a *dørk* from Århus from about 1200 was equipped with "finger-holes" and had a carved gaming-board showing that the men had an opportunity to pass the time on board with some amusement.

Skuldelev 2

Århus

Oars

The long rows of oars were the most characteristic feature of the warship in the Viking Age. The oars made the ship extra-manoeuvrable and able to move even when there was no wind to exploit.
This was a tactical advantage in particular – on longer stretches it was always the sail that was used. Oar-propelled warships remained of significance in warfare far down into the medieval period, not least in England and France.

The use of oars instead of paddles was introduced into Scandinavia around the time of the Birth of Christ. This marked a great advance because the rowers could now use more of their muscles for the propulsion of the ship. At the same time the power of propulsion was no longer transferred to the ship through the body of the rower but directly from oar to ship.

In the oldest Nordic rowing vessels the oars lay in *keiper*, tholepins, that were fixed to the gunwale. It was not until the early Viking Age that the planks in the sides of the ships began to be fitted with oar-holes. This made it possible to build the ships taller and hence more seaworthy. The oar-hole planks in the oldest ships were made of oak. Since this section of the ship was not preserved in Skuldelev 2, in the SEA STALLION we chose to use ash wood for it, as had been used for the oar-hole plank in the smaller warship Skuldelev 5. Ash is a type of wood that is not easily split.

It is important that the oars have the correct length and weight distribution so that it is possible to row with them for hours. In order to find the correct design of the oars for the SEA STALLION, we made an experimental setup and trials showed that 4.5 m was the best length for most of the oars. The shapes of the shank and the hand-grip of the oars were modelled on the ship-find from Gokstad.

The shape of the oarblades was copied from finds from the harbour in Hedeby.

The finds from Hedeby also showed that oars had been made of pine and alderwood. An oarblade that was found in the Skuldelev-barrier – but which need not necessarily have belonged to any of the ships there – was also made of alderwood. The SEA STALLION's oars are all made of pine, which is both light and supple and which grew in the forests of eastern Ireland in the eleventh century.

It is important to be able to close the oar-holes when the ship is under sail. This is done with an oar-hole cover and the model for the SEA STALLION's cover also comes from Hedeby.

Hedeby

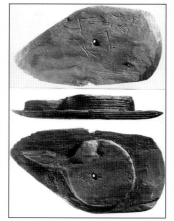

Hedeby

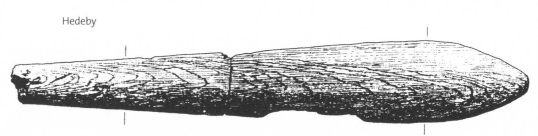

The keelson and the mast partner

In the centre of the ship there is an arrangement for holding the heel of the mast in position and bearing the weight of the rigging. This consists of the keelson, which has been joggled over the floor-timbers, and of the mast partner, which is positioned at the level of the thwarts. Two older, rather rude words for this contraption are known from the medieval sagas. Here the keelson is known as *kællingen* 'the old woman' and the mast partner as *kløften* 'the cleavage' – perhaps everyday nautical language that has found its way into contemporary literature. The keelson and mast partner also act as important reinforcements in the hull.

The keelson in the SEA STALLION is 14.1 m long and made as an exact copy of the fully preserved keelson from Skuldelev 2. It consists of two pieces, assembled with a hooked scarf, which is good at withstanding tension. In the middle the keelson has a marked thickening which leaves room for the mast step. Just in front of it a sturdy branch from the trunk from which the keelson has been shaped forms a strong arm whose end is firmly fixed to the bottommost beam in the mast frame. In this way the shipbuilder has ensured that the keelson could not be upset. When building the SEA STALLION it was no easy task to find a suitable tree for this particular purpose.

The keelson is fitted down on top of the floor-timbers and fastened with elegant knees to these. It is characteristic for the Viking ships that there are no direct nails between the keelson and the floor-timbers.

Several finds of keelsons from the Viking Age are preserved but no mast partners from large longships like Skuldelev 2. Two finds from the ninth century, one in the Gokstad ship and one from Århusbugten, have in combination with functional requirements determined the design of the SEA STALLION's keelson. While the oldest mast partners were apparently short and open at the one end, that from Gokstad was longer and closed at both ends. We therefore chose to make a long, closed mast partner for the SEA STALLION, which could at the same time serve as reinforcement for the longship in its central section. The mast partner is cut down above the thwarts and held in position from the sides by small knees.

The mast partner steers the mast when it is raised or lowered. When the mast has been raised, the oblong hole in the mast partner is closed with a mast coak. When this is fitted, the mast partner also supports the mast when the ship is under sail and relieve the pressure on the cordage of the rigging.

Keelson in the SEA STALLION

Mast partner in the Gokstad ship

Keelson in Skuldelev 2

The mast and the sail

The SEA STALLION's sail is 112 m², that is as big as a medium-sized bungalow. It is made of flax and carried on a yard that is hauled up in the centrally placed mast. All Viking ships were rigged in this way – just like all other Northern European sailing ships right down to about 1400. Even in the twentieth century such single square sails were employed, for example in Norway, and studies of this tradition have been important for the reconstruction of the sail of the Vikings.

Although nothing has been preserved of the rigging of Skuldelev 2, it has been possible to give a good idea of what it must have looked like, by studying the proportions of the ship and comparing it with other better preserved finds. In several of the Skuldelev ships many of the places where the rigging has been fastened to the hull have survived and this has made it possible to calculate, for example, the breadth of the sail. The height of the sail is more difficult to determine but over 20 years' experience sailing with reconstructions of the ships from the Skuldelev find has shown that the basic principles behind the rigging of traditional square-sailed

ships in Scandinavia are the same as they were for the eleventh-century Viking ships.

The diameter of the mast of Skuldelev 2 can be measured from the mast step but many of the other details in the rigging of the SEA STALLION have been inspired by other finds. The masthead is modelled after Scottish and Irish examples, while the parrel – the sliding loop that holds the sail in to the mast when sailing – is based on a find from Oseberg. The shrouds, which are the mast's supporting ropes in the sideways direction, are fastened to straps in the the side of the ship with the help of shroud-pins. They make it possible for the ropes to be loosened

and tightened and they have been made on the basis of finds from Fribrødre river. The many blocks and tackles have been constructed on the model of finds from Hedeby and Gokstad.

The Vikings used different materials for their sails. The two most significant were probably flax and wool. Flax is a plant-fibre and this gives a light and strong sail. It has two disadvantages as sailcloth – it rots rather easily and it is hard work to collect the fibres from the flax-plant. Wool also gives a light and strong sail but also a more elastic one and it does not rot. It makes greater demands of the surface treatment, however, than does the flax sail in order to become sufficiently impervious.

Dublin

Hedeby

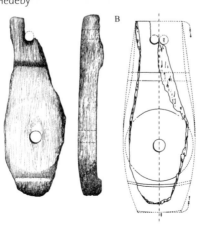

Norway

The cordage

About 2,200 m of cordage has gone to fitting out the SEA STALLION. By far the most of this is found in the rigging, where it serves to keep the mast in position and to manoeuvre the sail. The cordage in the SEA STALLION has been handmade of hemp and each individual piece of rope has been adapted to the particular function that it has to serve. The selection of hemp was for reasons of safety – the Vikings would undoubtedly have used cordage of lime-bast.

Most of the energy that the 112 m² - sail intercepts from the wind is lead through the cordage of the rigging down into the hull, where it gives steerage way and stability. A piece of rope that has been torn apart can, if the worst comes to the worst, end in shipwreck. That is why the SEA STALLION sails with a pilot rig of hemp instead of the rig of lime-bast that was probably borne by Skuldelev 2. Hemp rope is almost twice as strong as lime-bast rope and it is a material with which we have become familiar and which we know how to keep in good repair. The Viking Ship Museum has carried out experiments with rigs of lime-bast but we still dare not risk using it for a ship of this size.

All rigging consists of strands that are laid together to form cordage. If the raw material consists of thin fibres, these are first spun to form yarn that can then be twisted together into strands. If the material consists of coarse fibres, such as bast or skin, the strands are twisted from the raw material directly. The many kilometres of yarn for the SEA STALLION were spun mechanically and then twisted together to strands on a traditional ropewalk and the strands then laid together to produce cordage. Experiments have shown that lime bast was treated differently, being laid together by hand. It is therefore expensive to make lime-bast cordage today.

Lime bast was the most frequently employed material for cordage in the Viking Age but not the only one. Hair from horsetails was used, and experiments have shown that this yields a very springy cordage that does not absorb water. Animal skin has also been used. Walrus skin in particular produced a very strong cordage that was popular for maritime use. Hemp may also have been used – the plant was at all events known to the Vikings – but since hemp rots quickly under ground, it has rarely been preserved. Written sources reveal that at the latest in the 13th century hemp rope was common.

Roskilde 2

The tacking boom

The *tacking boom* or *beitiáss* is a stout pole that was used for steering and holding in position the foremost, bottom corner of the sail when sailing. Its one end rests in an *ásslag*, that is a pole support, which sits on the inside of the side of the ship, while its other end is fastened to the opposite side of the ship with a split piece of rope, an *ássdreng*. With the aid of the tacking boom it is possible surely and precisely to manoeuvre the foremost part of the sail and to distribute the great forces from here to the forepart of the vessel.

Old Norse *beita* means to beat up against the wind – to sail by the wind, we say today – and it is one of the few technical terms associated with sailing that we know from written sources in the Viking Age. An *áss* is a horizontal piece of timber – e.g. a beam in a roof – and the meaning of the word *beitiáss* is thus a horizontal piece of wood which is used when sailing by the wind. The word is known in the medieval period in various forms from France and England and from the Nordic countries including Iceland, and its dissemination therefore corresponds more or less with the spread of the clinker-built ship. No certain

archaeological find of a *beitiáss* has yet been made but in two ships from the Viking Age, the Gokstad ship and Skuldelev 1, fittings – *ásslög* – have been found in which the one end of the boom could be secured when it was in use. Examinations of these finds – and trial voyages with reconstructed ships equipped with *beitiáss* – have increased our knowledge of the function of the *beitiáss* and its mode of operation. The Gokstad ship was a combined rowing and sailing ship built in southern Norway shortly before 900. Here the bearings for the boom are preserved in both sides of the vessel. They sit on the inside of the side of the ship

slightly before the mast and they each have two recesses. Skuldelev 1 is a large cargo-ship that is contemporary with Skuldelev 2. Here the one *ásslag* is lacking but the other one is well preserved. It is made of lime and has three recesses. It is only the last of these that has been used for the *beitiáss*. The two in front have been used for longer poles, booms that were used when the wind came more from abaft and it was desirable for the sail to be distended further. Presumably Skuldelev 2 would also have sailed with other booms but this is an experiment that we have yet to try with the SEA STALLION.

The SEA STALLION

Skuldelev 1

Gokstad

Rudder and rudder-frame

In the Viking Age the rudder was a *balance rudder*, which was placed at the side of the ship. If it was correctly shaped and fitted – and the ship was otherwise properly trimmed and rigged – the helmsman needed no more strength to operate the rudder than was required to overcome the resistance in its two bearings. Under more abrupt manoeuvres, however, as when the ship was to be turned, the sail could also be of use – and, if necessary, the oars.

Until the middle of the twelfth century sea-going ships in Northern Europe were all steered with the help of so-called *side-rudders*. These were fixed to the rear of the ship on the right-hand side, which was therefore referred to as the starboard "steering-side". Neither the rudder nor the parts of the ship to which it had been fastened have been preserved in Skuldelev 2 but a number of other finds show what it may have looked like. Among the Danish finds there are two rudders in particular, from Vorså and from Hevringe Flak, which are considered to belong to the Viking Age. They are characteristic in having a small tail at the bottom on the afterside of the rudder blade, a feature which we also find on the Bayeux

Tapestry and which can therefore date this shape to the time of Skuldelev 2. The Vorså rudder – which the Viking Ship Museum has had good experience with during previous experiments – has thus been selected as the model for the SEA STALLION's rudder. On the Norwegian Viking ships from Oseberg and Gokstad and on the Danish Ellingå ship from the twelfth century we can study how the side-rudder was faste-ned to the side of the ship with a wicker-band that is passed through a rudder-boss, a wooden-block on the outer side of the ship. Then the wicker-band is passed through the side of the ship and several times round the rud-der-frame, a particularly strong frame in the rear of the ship. Here it can be

tightened with wedges so that the rudder is pulled firmly in against the rudder-boss. The wicker-band could be made of various materials – on the Oseberg ship it was made of pine, while in a rudder-frame from the Fribrødre river in Falster remains of an oaken-band have been found. On the SEA STALLION we have used tarred hemp rope. The upper part of the rudder-stock is held firmly in a bearing that has been hewn out of the outer side of the gunwale. A strap – on the Gokstad ship made of plaited lea-ther – ensures that the rudder-stock is pressed into the bearing.

Vorså

Fribrødre

Ellingå

The materials

The construction of the SEA STALLION has shown how many different resources, in the form of materials, human-beings and knowledge, that the building of a longship demanded. The forest was a particularly important provider of raw materials – but agriculture also contributed with indispensable materials for the production of sail and caulking, while minerals had to be dug out of the earth to produce the iron that has kept the ship together.

In all up to about 350 m³ of timber has gone to the construction of Skuldelev 2:

- For planks: 14 oaks, 8-10m in height, 1 m in diameter at chest height
- For the planks with oarports: 4 ashes, 10 m in height, 35 cm in diameter at chest height
- For the keel, stems, keelson and mast partners: 6 oaks, 8-10 m in height, 50-70 cm in diameter at chest height
- For the stringers: 3 oaks, 12 m in height, 60 cm in diameter at chest height
- For the frames: 285 pieces of naturally grown curved timber of oak
- For oars, mast, yard and spars: 50 pines, 5-13 m in height, 30-35 cm in diameter at chest height
- For treenails: 10 willows, 20-25 cm in diameter at chest height

- For cordage: bast from approx. 4,500 m lime branches of the thickness of an arm
- For tar: approx. 18 m³ pine roots and pinewood
- For charcoal for iron extraction and smithing: approx. 130 tons, or 150 m³ wood.

In addition approx. 3 tons of ore was dug out to produce 450-500 kg iron. To make the sail were used 200 kg flax or wool. For special pieces of cordage there were doubtless employed horsetails, perhaps as many as 600. Finally, dyestuffs and linseed oil were used for decorating the ship.

All the materials for Skuldelev 2 can have been obtained locally. Oak, ash, willow and lime were found around Dublin and in the neighbouring Wicklow Mountains. These yielded pinewood for the production of tar and for the oars, mast, yard and spars, and ore for the extraction of iron – unless the deposits of bog iron even nearer to hand were exploited. Both wool and flax for the sail could have been produced locally and linseed oil could have been extracted from the flax plants. The dyestuff ochre was found in the subsoil and woad had been introduced long before as a cultivated plant. Dublin was a significant trading place in the eleventh century and it is therefore possible that some commodities such as iron and dyestuffs had been imported

The craftsmen

The building of a longship demanded many different kinds of knowledge. In addition to expert boatbuilders it took smiths, ropemakers, weavers, sailmakers, painters, tar-burners, charcoal-burners, craftsmen who could extract iron, as well as folk to fell and transport timber, as well as to make flax and wool. There were no saws or machine-power and much time was expended. Altogether it must have taken about 50,000 hours to build Skuldelev 2.

The construction of the SEA STALLION showed that the actual building of the ship required about 27,000 man-hours. At the beginning of the 13th century Snorri Sturluson described the building of Olav Tryggvason's longship ORMR INN LANGI and named a number of the different jobs which were involved. If we divide up the man-hours on the SEA STALLION in the same categories, we get the following picture:

Master builder: 500 hours
Stem smith: 1,000 hours
Boatbuilders: 10,000 hours
Woodmen and assistants: 14,000 hours
Workers to clench the nails: 1,000 hours

In addition, however, there was much other work to be done that also took longer in the Viking Age than today. Provisionally we reckon that a further 13,000 man hours would have been spent on making tar, the sail and cordage, and on the transport of as much as 30 tons of partially hewn planks and pieces of timber which could first be completed on the building-site. In addition, the extraction of iron represents a significant workload. Approx. 130 tons of wood had to be burned to charcoal in order to roast and smelt three tons of iron ore and subsequently forge the iron pure. Farmers had to cultivate flax or breed

sheep in order to produce the material for the sailcloth, as well as to produce linseed oil from the flax. Dyestuffs had to be collected and prepared. Altogether the building of just a single large longship took perhaps 50,000 man hours or 15-20 years' work. A ship like Skuldelev 2 could at all events only have been used by a man who had manifold resources at his disposition – with a crew of 65 men it would have cost 5-6 men's work for a year just to man the ship for a voyage of one month.

The tools

The qualities of a Viking ship arise in the interplay between craftsman, materials and tools. At the same time the tools mean a great deal for how long it takes to build the ship and how expensive it will therefore be to do so. In order to achieve the correct result, both with respect to the qualities of the SEA STALLION and with respect to reconstructing Skuldelev 2's "price" in the form of man-hours, we employed copies of tools from the Viking Age in the course of the building.

There are many finds of tools from the Viking Age. Craftsmen were often buried with some of their tools, other tools were lost or forgotten during work, and some were deliberately thrown into the water or buried. One of the most important finds of tools from the Viking Age is the Mästermyr chest, a wooden chest that was discovered in 1936 on the island of Gotland in the Baltic. It has been dated to the 11th century and contains over 100 well-preserved objects, in particular tools for smithing and woodwork.

Illustrative material is also important. On the Bayeux tapestry the construction of William the Conqueror's fleet is displayed with many details, while the medieval pictures of the building of Noah's Ark give us an impression of shipbuilding in other Christian parts of Europe.

The most important tools in Viking-Age shipbuilding were the axes and the augers. With the axes timber and planks could be hewn and with the augers thousands of holes were made for the ship's nails to be knocked through. Different axes were used for different purposes – heavy, sturdy axes with short blades for felling and rough hewing, asymmetrical axes with the long edge ground only on the one side for smoothing planks, and small one-handed axes for the precise shaping of floor-timbers and other woodwork. Planes were only used on the most splendid vessels, while most ships had decorative mouldings along the edges of the planks and timbers, produced with the aid of a scraping device.

One tool, the saw, is lacking altogether in Viking-Age shipbuilding. Although the tool was known – one instance was found in the Mästermyr chest – no trace has been found of its use on the ship-finds. Perhaps contemporary saws were still too small to be of use in a trade that had been developing the axe as its most important tool for one thousand years.

Hedeby Bayeux   Sæbø

Where is it in the ship?

AFT

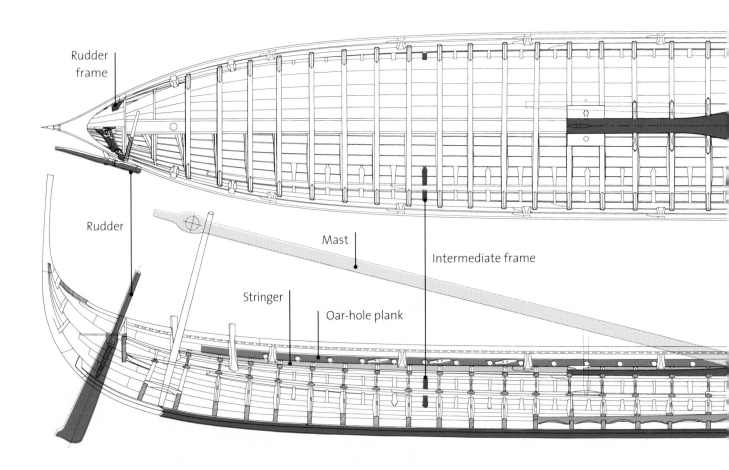

Rudder frame

Rudder

Mast

Intermediate frame

Stringer

Oar-hole plank

FORE

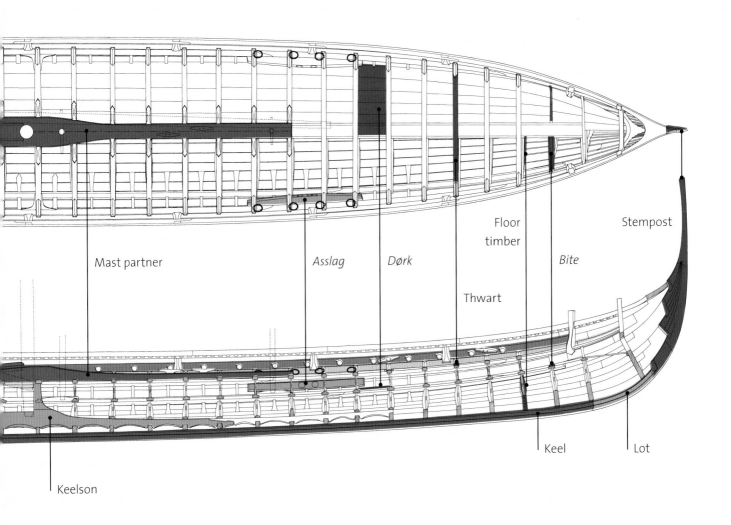

Mast partner

Asslag

Dørk

Floor
timber

Stempost

Thwart

Bite

Keelson

Keel

Lot

Why do we go on trial voyages?

In July 2007 the SEA STALLION is sailing from Roskilde with course for Dublin – and in the summer of 2008 the return voyage will go back to Roskilde. On both occasions the voyage will use the ship's own means of propulsion, oars and sail, and the crew will consist of 65 men and women, largely volunteers who are using weeks of their holidays for the trip. Why do they do this?

For more that 20 years the Viking Ship Museum has carried out voyages with reconstructions of the Skuldelev ships. The aim has been to find out how the Viking ships sailed: How swift were they? How seaworthy? Could they only sail in fair weather and with a following wind or could they also keep themselves free of a rockbound coast in an onshore wind and stormy weather? How many people were necessary to sail them? How many people could be carried on board – and with how heavy or bulky a cargo? These are all questions that, if they are answered, will help to throw light on how the Scandinavians in the Viking Age came to be of such great signifi-

cance as warriors, merchants and colonizers.

The Viking Ship Museum carries out two kinds of experimental voyages. The one kind is sea trials in which we investigate the ship's technical qualities. What is the greatest speed for sail and oars? How close can it sail to the wind? How long does it take to turn the ship or bring it to a standstill and how much space does it need to do this? The technical qualities are good for making comparisons between the ships if we are considering them as sailing machines. On the other hand, however, they are not very useful for throwing light on the significance of the ships as transport tools because

they can take account neither of the human factor nor of the instability of the weather. A rowing- or sailing-ship cannot sail further or more swiftly than the crew can keep going and it will be necessary to wait until there is more wind, or less, or coming from a different direction. That is why the Viking Ship Museum also carries out experimental voyages, where a ship performs comparatively long voyages under as realistic conditions as possible with respect to practicality and security. To a much higher degree than the top speeds of the sea trials, these experimental voyages give an impression of how swiftly and how far the Vikings could travel in their ships.

ROAR EGE

OTTAR

THE SEA STALLION FROM GLENDALOUGH

With the Sea Stallion across the North Sea

With a sailing ship one can never be quite certain where the journey is going to lead. The plan, however, is that the voyage in 2007 will go from Roskilde via Southern Norway across the North Sea to Orkney. Then it will continue around the Atlantic coast of Scotland down into the Irish Sea and Dublin. The route in 2008 will go from Dublin south around England past Hastings. With a southwesterly wind behind us we shall go up through the North Sea until we can perhaps set our course into Limfjorden and across the Kattegat to Roskilde.

The Vikings in Ireland had close contacts over the sea with Norway, Denmark and the Scandinavian settlements along the coasts of England and Scotland. Both the route north and the route south round the British Isles were employed and for journeys between Denmark and Ireland there is no great difference in the lengths of the two. It was probably other considerations that decided the choice. The weather in particular can have been an important factor. Today easterly winds are more common in the spring than in the autumn, where south-westerly winds prevail. Similar patterns a thousand years ago can have determined when and where the expeditions were planned. The voyage of the SEA STALLION will try out both routes, the one around Scotland probably being the tougher of the two. Here the ship can expect to meet rather large waves on its way across the North Sea and along the north coast of Scotland between Orkney and the Hebrides. The SEA STALLION will have to do just as the Vikings did – wait for the days when wind and weather ensure the safety of the voyage.

The return journey will take place well within the edge of the continental shelf and very large waves are unlikely to occur. The chance of getting a favourable wind is also greater than on the journey out. The voyage will not, however, be without its challenges. When the ship leaves the Irish Sea it will have the entire Atlantic on its starboard and it has to get round Land's End, the sharpest corner of Cornwall. After this follows a voyage through one of the world's most frequented waters, the English Channel, with its strong tidal currents. Not until after passing Dover will the sea open out again and become the North Sea, which by that time will seem to be almost homely.

On the voyage the investigations of the seaworthiness of the SEA STALLION under sail and oars will be intensified in the very waters where the original ship once sailed. We hope that they will provide the answers to why the Vikings in Ireland in 1042 built Skuldelev 2 as they did.

How do we measure?

How do we study the voyage of a ship over the sea? It is no easy task because a ship under sail is a complex mechanism that consists of the vessel itself and its qualities, of the weather and the waves and, not least, of the crew, their know-how and their reaction to the influences upon them. The research programme for the voyage of the SEA STALLION has been put together from a large number of studies that in conjunction with each other should throw light on these different aspects.

On the surface the SEA STALLION resembles its 1,000-year-old model. If we look at the inside of the ship, however, we find a tangle of cables that link the vast amount of electronic equipment on board which registers the movements of the ship and of wind and weather. With the help of satellite navigation the precise position of the ship is registered every tenth of a second and the air temperature is also measured and registered electronically, while an echo sounder measures the depth of the water, a log measures the speed through the water and the electronic compass keeps a check on the course steered. All the data is collected in a "black box" and selected data is transmitted to land every hour via a radio satellite.

While on board ship the crew is keeping several different logbooks. The skipper and the mate note down regularly whether the ship is being sailed or rowed, what manoeuvres are carried out, whether the sail is reefed, how much the ship is heeling, and other matters concerning the navigation of the ship. The boatswain goes through the ship each day to note wear and tear and any damage to hull, rudder and rigging, just as changes in the distribution of the ballast are registered continually. Five *rum*-foremen, spread around the ship, take notes every day about events and experiences within the section of the ship for which they are responsible. Account is kept of the food consumed on board and a nurse keeps a journal over the state of health of the crew.

Safety is a topic of central importance for an open ship with 65 people on board and it has priority above all else. The SEA STALLION is accompanied all the time by another ship on its voyage to Dublin. The ship is equipped with radar, an emergency radio and life-rafts, and each member of the crew has a survival suit – should the worst come to the worst. The greatest degree of safety that the crew of the SEA STALLION can attain, however, is as in the case of the crew of Skuldelev 2 one thousand years ago – with the aid of foresight, responsibility and good seamanship.

Our first experiences

Before the voyage to Dublin the SEA STALLION has been on 16 voyages with a total of 84 days sailing since it was launched in September 2004. We therefore already know something about how swiftly and how well the ship can sail. The most significant experiences were made on a trial voyage from Roskilde to Oslo in 2006, where the ship both met its hitherto biggest waves and made its hitherto longest voyage without going ashore.

How quickly could a large longship sail – and how far could it go? No one knows as yet but the first trials with the SEA STALLION indicate a vessel that could sail quickly and far but which made great demands on its crew. With its long waterline and narrow cross section the ship accelerates quickly and has so far achieved speeds of up to 11 knots – about 20 km per hour – measured in a fresh wind. On longer stretches it is possible to keep up speeds of about the half of that, and with a hardy crew and a favourable wind the ship can make the voyage from Sjælland to the Oslo Fjord in less than two days, or from Jutland to England in just three days. Experience has also shown, however, that

the very cramped conditions on board a longship wear out a modern crew – it is quite simply difficult to get enough sleep. Although Viking-Age sea-warriors were more hardy than we are today, the health of the crew would also then have limited the speed of the longships and made it necessary to hold breaks for rest on route.

The longships can also be rowed – but how quickly? The preliminary results with the SEA STALLION show that the speed for oars is about 5 knots or less than 10 km per hour – and that only for shorter distances, and not against the wind or in large waves. With only every other oar manned the speed only drops slightly, because there is then more room to row in – and the

rowers can also take turns to row and hence row for longer periods. The oars have, however, hardly been the method of propulsion on the long voyages but simply a means of placing oneself in a favourable position according to the direction of the wind or the presence of enemy ships.

The seaworthiness of the SEA STALLION appears to be good. Under full sail the ships can sail about 65° to the wind, the drift included. This means that it is among the most well-sailing of our replicas of Viking ships, and that it was able to keep itself free of the coast in an onshore wind – an important quality for a sailing ship without an engine.

Who is supporting the project?

The construction of the SEA STALLION and the trial voyage to Dublin have been made possible by contributions from a large number of foundations, authorities and sponsors. The Viking Ship Museum in Roskilde would like to take this opportunity once more to thank them for the backing and enthusiasm that has been shown to us by the museum's supporters.

Foundations:	Sponsors:	Official support:
TUBORGFONDET	JD CONTRACTOR APS SUBMARINE DENMARK · SINCE 1972	Kultur MINISTERIET
Skibsreder Carsten Brebøl's Almennyttige Fond		
Carlsbergs Mindelegat for Brygger J.C. Jacobsen	NORDEN	KUL TUR ARV
Augustinus Fonden	VIKING LIFE-SAVING EQUIPMENT	The Department of Arts, Sport and Tourism
Knud Højgaards Fond	FURUNO Professional Maritime Electronics	ROSKILDE KOMMUNE
Dronning Margrethes og Prins Henriks Fond	Thrane & Thrane	Roskilde Amt
Nykredits Fond		
Familien Hede Nielsens Fond	RIR·REVISION	mcmurdo
Konsul Georg Jorck og hustru Emma Jorck's Fond	RIFF SKILTEFABRIK	bp
	IMERCO Ro's Torv Roskilde	FOSEN FOLKEHØGSKOLE
Brødrene Hartmanns Fond	Toms	SAS Scandinavian Airlines
Det Obelske Familiefond	Frisport®	SPEJDER SPORT

Welcome on board! The Sea Stallion from Glendalough
A Viking longship recreated

Copyright © 2007 by The Viking Ship Museum
Second impression 2007
All rights reserved

Text and editing: Jan Bill, Søren Nielsen, Erik Andersen, Tinna Damgård-Sørensen
Translation: Gillian Fellows-Jensen
Special thanks to: Judith Jesch, Heid Gjøstein Resi, Brian Scott.

Layout: Mette Kryger
Printed in Denmark by Nofoprint A/S

ISBN: 978-87-85180-41-4

Publications by:
The Viking Ship Museum
Vindeboder 12
DK-4000 Roskilde, Denmark

Viking Ship Museum books can be ordered online via
www.vikingshipmuseum.dk or www.oxbowbooks.com

Photos and drawings:

Werner Karrasch, the Viking Ship Museum

and

Archäologisches Landesmuseum, Schleswig: p. 25 Tar trough Hedeby; p. 37 Hedeby (right); p. 41 Hedeby;
Bergen Museum: p. 16 Bergen
Biopix: p. 27 Ochre, Flax, Woad.
Vibeke Bischoff, the Viking Ship Museum: p. 9 Torso reconstruction; p. 10 (center left)
Bodleian Library, Oxford: p. 21 Noah's Ark
Dreamtime: p. 59 (left)
Morten Gøthche, the Viking Ship Museum: p. 54-55
Gabriel Hildebrand, Statens historiska museum, Stockholm: p. 17 Söderala.
Werner Karrasch, Archäologisches Landesmuseum, Schleswig: p. 13 Hedeby; p. 31 Hedeby;
Kr. Kielland: p. 41 Norway
Ole Klindt Jensen, *Vikingetidens kunst*: p. 17 Källunge
Kulturhistorisk Museum, Oslo: p. 15 Fortun stave church; p. 17 Tingelstad; p. 19 Oseberg; p. 39 Mast partner, Gokstad; p. 45 Gokstad;
National Museum of Denmark: p. 6; p. 8; p. 10 (upper right, center left, lower left and right); p. 15 Skuldelev 2; p. 23 Skuldelev 2;
    p. 29 Skuldelev 2; p. 31 Skuldelev 2, p. 33 Skuldelev 2; p. 35 Skuldelev 2; p. 47 Ellingå, Vorså
National Museum of Ireland, Dublin: p. 41 Dublin
Anne Stalsberg, Vitenskapsmuseet, Trondheim: p. 20 Gaudalen
La Tapisserie de Bayeux: p. 19 Bayeux; p. 27 Bayeux; p. 53 Bayeux
Per Pejstrup, Copenhagen: p. 10 (upper left)
Jan Riishede, the Viking Ship Museum: p. 7 (left)
Hans Skov, Moesgård Museum: p. 35 Århus
Tourism Ireland: p. 19 Glendalough; p. 59 (center)
The Viking Ship Museum: p. 31 Roskilde 6; p. 47 Fribrødre
Wikinger Museum Haithabu: p. 37 Hedeby (left)